A Director's Guide

Customer relationship management

HOW DIRECTORS CAN BUILD BUSINESS THROUGH IMPROVED CUSTOMER RELATIONS

Editor, Director Publications: Tom Nash
Managing Editor: Lesley Shutte
Consultant Editor: Marc Beishon
Production Manager: Victoria Davies
Design: Halo Design
Commercial Director: Simon Seward
Managing Director: Andrew Main Wilson
Chairman: George Cox

Published for the Institute of Directors
and Oracle Corporation UK Ltd
by Director Publications Ltd
116 Pall Mall London SW1Y 5ED

Editorial: 020 7766 8910
Production: 020 7766 8960
Sponsorship: 020 7766 8885
Copy sales: 020 7766 8766
Facsimile: 020 7766 8990

YOURS TO HAVE AND TO HOLD
BUT NOT TO COPY

The publication you are reading is protected by copyright law. This means that the publisher could take you and your employer to court and claim heavy legal damages if you make unauthorised photocopies from these pages. Photocopying copyright material without permission is no different from stealing a magazine from a newsagent.

The Copyright Licensing Agency (CLA) issues licences to bring photocopying within the law. It has designed licensing services to cover all kinds of special needs in business, education and government.

If you take photocopies from books, magazines and periodicals at work your employer should be licensed with the CLA. Make sure you are protected by a photocopying licence.

The Copyright Licensing Agency
90 Tottenham Court Road
London W1P 0LP
Tel: 020 7436 5931 Fax: 020 7436 3986

Director Publications Ltd
116 Pall Mall
London SW1Y 5ED

Kogan Page Ltd
120 Pentonville Road
London N1 9JN

© Director Publications Ltd 1999

British Library Cataloguing in Publication Data
A CIP record for this book is available from the British Library
ISBN 0 7494 3295 0

Printed and bound in Great Britain

Contents

IN YOUR ORGANISATION, ARE EACH OF YOUR
CUSTOMERS UNIQUE?

At PricewaterhouseCoopers, our Customer Relationship Management team can help businesses **understand** their customers and **achieve** their goals.

For further information please contact Rod Street on 0171 212 8757.

www.pwcglobal.com

Join us. Together we can change the world.

The CRM challenge

George Cox, Director General, Institute of Directors

Customer relationship management (CRM) has received so much attention that it is in danger of being regarded as the guru-promoted solution to virtually every business problem.

It is not helped by the fact that vendors and consultants are applying a CRM label to almost everything in business – sales, marketing and service – and urging everyone to integrate all their systems, not only with each other, but also with new channels and concepts, especially the internet and e-commerce. In practice, to view CRM as either hype or an impenetrably complex issue is a huge mistake which could result in missing out on a major opportunity to transform customer understanding and expand relationships.

The fundamentals of good customer handling are as old as commerce itself. The ability to get to know the customer, to anticipate needs and to deliver great service is still alive and well in many small businesses today. What has changed is that technology now allows larger companies to follow the same approach.

Far from depersonalising the world, technology actually does the opposite. It makes it possible for a large organisation to deal with each customer as an individual. As organisations realise this and implement systems which progressively put this into practice, so customer-focus and service excellence become the basis for competition. The problem for the larger business is not the lack of possibility, it is the twin issues of how to select the right way forward and how to implement the necessary change. Moreover, it is not a static issue: experience is growing rapidly, customer expectations are rising and the technology is always moving forward. The possibilities grow more exciting by the day – as does the danger of not keeping up with the competition.

This Director's Guide explains clearly how CRM can be deployed using today's thinking and technology.

Understanding our customers' needs

Ian A Smith, Vice President and Managing Director, UK & Ireland Oracle Corporation UK Ltd

As we approach the Millennium, there has never been a better time to reflect on how we behave, individually and collectively, in our personal lives as well as professionally. Inevitably, such introspection encourages us to examine our relationships with others – family, friends, colleagues, employees, business partners and customers.

Appropriately, therefore, we are all focusing on the most important of all commercial relationships – the relationship with our customers. The term Customer Relationship Management (CRM) has certainly become part of current business vocabulary, and it is essential that we understand its many different manifestations, and the tools available to help us address this vital issue.

Each customer is different and therefore our relationship with them needs to be tailored to match their needs. This requires a flexible approach that will allow us to map our organisation consistently and competitively to our customers' demands in terms of products, services and channels.

If we understand who our customers are (or indeed, who we would like to be our customers), identify the segments within our customer base and understand the needs of these groups, we will be in a position to create products and services that can satisfy the customer.

But we must beware of commoditisation – of services, of products and worst of all, of customers. Commoditisation devalues all of these. We need to ensure that we focus on value.

It isn't so long ago that the local shop owner was able to

relate to us on a personal basis. He would know all that there was to know about our families, how we worked, how we played, how we worshipped and so on. He would be able to judge our moods and perhaps anticipate our needs – stocking goods that we might not even know we wanted – adding value to his offerings.

We need to recreate this personal relationship with all of our most valuable customers – creating the opportunities for cross-selling of our own offerings or those of our partners – and focus on the cost control aspects with less valuable segments. To do this, we need accurate profitability assessment, and analysis of behaviour patterns and preferences which can only really be achieved in today's high volume environments through the application of technology across the business.

The articles in this guide cover CRM from many different angles and I sincerely hope that you find them useful in the development of your own company's approach to relating to your customer base. Wishing you every success.

Who you trust in business is more than a matter of faith

Cap Gemini Group is the largest European IT services and business consultancy company.

Imagination, trust and partnership are fundamental elements of our culture. They are the core values that define how we work and are central to everything we do.

Through our Customer Relationship Management practice we help clients to know their customers, to target them with the right proposition through the right channels, to sell to them and to service them.

We do what we say, we do it well, and we deliver beyond expectation. That's why so many leading companies place their trust in us.

CAP GEMINI
You can contact us today on
Tel: 0800 120123,
Fax: 0171 434 8427

www.capgemini.com

Chapter 1

Building a business of delight

The techniques of modern marketing mean little unless part of a coherent CRM strategy. Adrian Payne, Professor and Director of the Centre for Relationship Marketing at Cranfield University, and Marc Beishon, business and technology writer, explain why

Customer relationship management, or CRM, has made a high-profile entry into the business vocabulary in the past year or so and promises to be a key strategic issue over the next decade.

There are compelling reasons why CRM should be addressed by organisations of all sizes. The techniques and technologies behind it can help increase customer satisfaction and, therefore, shareholder value. But for many companies, there is confusion as to what CRM is all about. To some, it is about a loyalty scheme, to others, a customer help desk. To some, it is about a relational database for key account management, to others, segmenting the customer base.

Relatively few organisations have an integrated approach that addresses all the key elements of CRM, while only a small number of businesses have a good idea of the role of information technology in implementing a successful strategy.

This chapter aims to define the goals of CRM and to explain how it intersects with both marketing and information technology.

THE THEORY OF CRM

So what exactly is CRM and what are its principal tenets? It has its roots in relationship marketing, a topic which was which first written about in the early 1980s.

Relationship marketing is considered by many of its proponents to be a major breakthrough in business thinking. Essentially, it advocates a radical shift in mindset, from focusing mostly on prospecting and winning new business to concentrating more on customer retention. This is of particular relevance in the mature markets that most businesses operate in.

Put simply, the argument is that customer retention is often far more important than customer acquisition. A relatively small increase in retention rates can result in a relatively big increase in profits. Signing up new business, on the other hand, can incur high costs and take several years to show a return.

This is not to say that customer acquisition is not important – it most certainly is – but that the right balance must be struck between the effort and expense spent on winning new business and that spent on retaining and developing existing customer relationships. This is where the vast majority of companies fail. Research by Professor Adrian Payne at Cranfield University suggests that as much as 80 per cent of UK companies are spending too much time, money and effort on acquisition, while 10 per cent have erred in the opposite direction, concentrating too heavily on retention strategies. That leaves just another 10 per cent, that have got the balance right.

THE VALUE OF CUSTOMER RETENTION

A good CRM strategy keeps the value of customer retention in a realistic perspective. Research by Bain & Co shows that a five percentage point increase in customer retention yields a profit, in net present value terms, of between 20 per cent and 125 per cent. Confirmation of this level of return comes from Deloitte Consulting, which in a recent study, *Making Customer Loyalty Real*, found that manufacturing companies that set clear targets for customer retention and make extra efforts to exceed them are on average 60 per cent more profitable than companies that do not focus on customer loyalty.

Although many managers are now familiar with findings of this type, Cranfield's research has shown that few actually know what the profit value of retention is in their own business. While the actual retention rate may be known, it is often very difficult to understand how changes in the rate affect profitability in your business and in your customer segments.

This is precisely the kind of question that a CRM strategy, backed up with the emerging development of CRM software tools, is able to tackle successfully.

RELATIONSHIPS AND HOW TO BUILD THEM

Like many good business strategies, CRM is based on common sense. While much of the theory about relationship marketing may be recent, the art and practice of relating to customers is not at all new. Even the earliest merchants knew how to visit customers and keep records. And a superb example of good CRM in practice can be seen in the humble corner shop.

A corner shop proprietor knows customers by name, knows what their likes and dislikes are, knows their creditworthiness, knows when they get paid (or when the pocket money comes in) and addresses them individually according to their status. He or she keeps in his or her memory what the customers have in their own minds and anticipates their needs.

Essentially, the main difference between the single corner shop keeper and the growing business is one of scale. What the proprietor keeps in his or her head the growing business must keep in a database; what the proprietor delivers through regular contact with individual customers – ie. a relationship – the growing business that is becoming remote from its customers must deliver through good marketing and customer management.

Good does not have to mean expensive. It is not money that differentiates the CRM winners from the losers. For companies such as Marks & Spencer and The Body Shop, public relations and word-of-mouth marketing have been very important: despite fairly low levels of advertising spend, their marketing has been highly effective. (Whatever M&S's current troubles, no-one can deny the strength of its historic relationship with the the public.) Many organisations have, despite heavy investment in marketing, achieved poor results; quite a number of financial services companies fall into this category.

CRM AND MARKETING STRATEGIES

How can companies be sure their marketing efforts will not be wasted? For one thing, they must have systems to measure the effectiveness of their marketing tools.

The marketing function may be the last bastion of inadequate and inappropriate metrics. Lord Leverhulme is reputed to have said: "Half the money I spend on advertising is wasted – the trouble is I never know which half it is."

This approach to marketing is no longer acceptable. Organisations would not tolerate an HR manager who recruited two people because he or she did not know which one would be better; or an operations director who built two plants because he was not sure which one would operate effectively.

Companies must have an approach that rejects ineffectual marketing and advertising. The main thing that distinguishes good a marketing strategy from weak marketing strategy, however, is the recognition that the relationship with the customer has to be continually managed. Traditional marketing activities that emphasise customer acquisition are no longer sufficient. A fundamental tenet of CRM is that the "real" marketing starts after the sale is over, not before the sale is completed.

According to Professor Payne: "CRM is the strategic process of identifying desirable customer segments, micro-segments or individual customers on a one-to-one basis and developing integrated programmes that maximise both value to the customer and the lifetime value of customers to the organisation through targeted customer acquisition, profit enhancing activities and retention. It utilises relationship marketing principles that are exploited through information, technology and front and back office applications". (See also the panel on Ovum's key CRM goals opposite, which present a further perspective.)

CRM AND INFORMATION TECHNOLOGY

In-depth, one-to-one customer knowledge is the essence of relationship marketing and CRM. Once their customer base reaches, say, 50, it is not practical for most companies to retain this customer

THE KEY GOALS OF CRM

A CRM strategy requires a holistic view of the customer by the organisation, and a holistic view of the organisation by the customer. These views improve the ability of an organisation to achieve its key goals:

- To determine the kind of customers it wants to attract, attain and retain;

- To determine what products, services and combinations thereof will be attractive to the most profitable customers;

- To attract, attain and retain its target profitable customers by better sales and support service;

- To provide the kind of service that will keep profitable customers satisfied and loyal.

Source: Ovum

knowledge without office aids. Those aids used to be paper-based records – now they are increasingly powerful computer programs. The fact that the cost of computing platforms has plummeted means the SME sector is now able to run more highly complex IT systems. Software branded with the CRM label is now available for the SME, showing that the CRM tools market is maturing.

The priority in the earlier years of the mass deployment of computing systems was to automate the operational functions of the business, such as accounts, stock control, manufacturing and so on. Now it is to look at "softer" disciplines. The rising expectations of both consumers and business-to-business customers have increased the need for CRM software.

The level of service and speed of turnaround common in the early 1980s for answering enquiries and shipping goods is not acceptable in most industries today.

The interest in CRM programs, as distinct from CRM as a topic, also stems from the downturn of the late 1980s: as economies went in and out of recession, new company models emerged that had IT at their core. First Direct bank and Direct Line Insurance, for example, built a new approach to customer service on the back of telecommunications and computing. Their technology is one of their most important CRM tools. IT also provides a vehicle for improved customer service. Thanks to the internet and online shopping, some UK supermarket customers, for example, now have the option of a home delivery service.

Technology is not just providing tools to aid CRM; it is making CRM a commercial necessity. In the new internet world, companies have to recognise that the customer is increasingly in the driving seat. With a much wider choice of vendors instantly available, customer service – indeed customer delight – is becoming a key differentiator between companies.

The rise of the internet and the growing use of call-centre technology mean companies must work harder at customer management if they are to appear as one "joined up" organisation from the outside. If they get passed around departments like a commercial football, customers will take their business elsewhere.

IMPLEMENTING TECHNOLOGICAL SOLUTIONS

No-one is pretending that a full CRM solution is an easy, short-term goal. In large corporations, the huge amount of "legacy" information and disparate sources of customer data can take considerable time to pull together.

The preferred route for many firms at present is to implement parts of an eventual CRM solution that they feel most comfortable with, such as a call centre dedicated to order taking and cross-selling, or a central repository for all customer data. Sometimes, a firm will have adopted so-called business intelligence software, which helps to identify patterns of customer behaviour.

In fact, a CRM solution could encompass a long list of both "front office" and "back office" systems, which are described elsewhere in this guide. The challenge is to identify which mix of techniques and systems are appropriate for a business. "Planned evolution" is a good way of summarising the approach required. This would see a gradual growth of new systems instead of the upheaval caused by a crisis management solution.

MODELLING TECHNIQUES

A good way to revisit a marketing strategy is to break down the acquisition-retention debate into more detail using sophisticated models – such as a Retentiongram model.

Traditionally, directors have found it difficult to determine the exact impact of customer retention in their businesses and how it varies across market segments and micro-segments. The Retentiongram model (developed by Adrian Payne and a colleague at Cranfield) enables the profit impact of changes in customer retention to be measured at the aggregate, segment and micro-segment levels. The model allows a trade-off to be made in the allocation of scarce organisational resources between strategies aimed at retaining existing customers and those concerned with attracting new customers. Choices can also be made about the relative emphasis to be placed on strategies for different customer segments.

The model enables calculation of the impact on profitability of a number of factors related to customer retention and acquisition. These factors, which represent the input variables to the model, include: the customer retention rate; the number of existing customers; the acquisition target for new customers; the cost of acquiring each customer; interest rates and the profit per customer per period. These input variables are used to calculate a range of output variables including: the total number of customers at defined periods in the future; the total profit at defined periods in the future; the net present value of a customer; and the net present value of the firm's future profits.

AIM HIGH

Remember, the starting point for adopting a new approach has to be a review of the existing one. Set your standards high: even if your customer management is rated as good, this will not be enough if your competitors are in the business of delight.

Chapter 2

Becoming a customer-focused company

Most businesses agree that the customer is king. But the majority of companies can still do more to become customer-focused. Paul Taylor, IT correspondent at the Financial Times, reports

STEP ONE

Identify the customer

The first step towards becoming a customer-focused company is to identify and define the customer. Only after the customer has been identified, can the company begin to define the customer relationship.

But, as business consultants will attest, many companies still have only a vague idea of who their customers are and many have never really considered the issue at all.

For retail and other organisations such as financial services firms that come into direct contact with the end user of the goods or services that they offer, identifying the customer may be fairly easy. They "touch" their customers directly, usually at the point of sale but also by other means such as advertising, direct-mail shots or, increasingly, via the internet.

These organisations should already have a pretty well defined "picture" of their customers and should know about their wants, needs and grumbles. But many do not. For example, banks always seem surprised by research studies that show high levels of customer dissatisfaction – a failure that ultimately exposes them to competition both from within and outside the sector.

Serving the secondary customer

There are many companies that deal primarily with intermediaries or are suppliers within a chain – they have both primary and secondary customers whom they need to identify. For example, a food manufacturer may supply supermarkets directly, but its ultimate customer is the shopper.

Similarly, a chemicals company may supply one of the ingredients used in making paint. Its customers are both the paint manufacturer and the end users. It needs to be "in touch" with both its customers and its customers' customers.

A classic example of a company that asked the question "who are our customers" and came up with some surprising answers is Intel, the giant US chipmaker. Ostensibly, as a component supplier Intel only had a relationship with intermediaries, in this case personal computer manufacturers. But it used pioneering and extremely effective marketing to build a direct relationship with end users. The "Intel Inside" campaign forged a direct relationship between Intel and PC users and enabled Intel to build customer loyalty and outmanoeuvre its rivals.

Similarly, the person paying for a product or service may not be the only or even most important customer. Consider toy manufacturers, sweet makers and comic publishers, for example. Often it will be parents or another adult buying the product, but that purchasing decision will often be driven by end-user pressure – in this case a child influenced by advertising and peer pressure in addition to his or her own previous experience.

Within companies, one department or division may be a supplier to another department or division and may face direct competition from potential external suppliers. This reality has been driven home in organisations that have chosen to outsource non-core operations, turning an internal supplier into an external supplier or partner competing directly with other potential suppliers.

Even the government has customers for every public service run by a government office – hospital patients, parents and social security recipients are all consumers of its services – and, of course, internal consumers.

STEP TWO

Collect, clean and store data

Many organisations have either failed to collect information about their customers over the years or have thrown it away because at the time it appeared useless and unimportant. As most retailers now recognise, all data – and that includes refunds, returned items and complaints – can be useful in building up a picture of a customer.

There are many sources for customer data. The most obvious is "point-of-sale". Information collected at the checkout counter or till can be particularly valuable if the purchase can be tied to an individual shopper via credit card details or customer loyalty schemes. Customer loyalty schemes usually require the cardholder to fill out a form, covering basic details such as name, address, age and so forth. This data can be tied to other information such as the frequency of shopping, time of day and distance travelled from home, as well as likes and dislikes based upon the till receipt. For a bank, the use of an Automated Teller Machine represents a chance to collect information about a customer, or a rival's customer.

Call centres are another important source of customer information and most call centre systems include a data capture element. However, the usefulness of vital information, particularly negative comments or complaints, is often overlooked. Within most organisations good news such as contract wins or customer praise travels fast, but bad news is often buried and never transmitted to those people who most need to know about it. If problems are kept hidden they can't be addressed. Enlightened organisations recognise this and place the highest value on the information collected by help desks, complaints departments and warrantee claims.

As electronic commerce gathers pace, the web is also proving to be a rich source of customer data. Online orders provide a wealth of detail about the customer, including names, addresses, payment methods and so forth. Sophisticated web tools can augment this with information such as which sites the customer has visited, how many times he or she visited the site before buying, etc.

Third-party sources of information

For those companies that do not have a direct relationship with the end user, it may be possible to reach information-sharing agreements with retailers or obtain "primary" information through customer market search, competitions or discount coupons.

While these primary sources of data are crucial to building up a full picture of the customer, it will usually be necessary to augment the basic data with other information, much of it available from third-party sources. This ranges from demographic material gleaned from census forms and other sources to "lifestyle" data collected by third parties.

Whatever the source of the data, it needs to be "cleaned" (the old adage "rubbish in, rubbish out" applies here) and prepared for storage – usually in a huge database called appropriately, a data warehouse. The data warehouse lies at the core of a customer relationship management system. It is the repository for all the data related to customers. Typically, it comprises both hardware and software tools and requires highly scaleable systems – some of the largest data warehouses built by retail giants such as Wal-Mart in the US now hold more that 20Tb (terabits) of data.

Pulling down vertical barriers

Building a data warehouse is an essential step in becoming a customer-focused company and developing what has been called a holistic or 360-degree view of a customer. One of the problems that many companies have is that customer data has been collected and stored across several parts of an organisation. So, for example, in a bank one department knows all about a customer's current account, but does not know that the individual also has a mortgage with the same organisation and is considering taking out an insurance policy with another division.

Building a common customer database is often at the core of an enterprise customer management strategy, which will typically also encompass sales support, marketing support, customer support – including call centres – and quality assurance. Despite this, a recent UK study published by KPMG Consulting revealed that only five per cent of companies currently possess an integrated central database. "Many companies are failing to exploit one of their most valuable assets – customer information," says Steve King, the KPMG partner responsible for customer management.

In many companies, information is stored in "information silos" that correspond to the vertical divisions within an organisation – which may be geographic, functional or according to product and product groups. The problem therefore, is that no one part of the business has a complete picture of the customer. Overcoming this is not just a matter of throwing technology at the issue. It may well involve changes in corporate culture, particularly in companies where individual fiefdoms have grown up and flourished.

Properly built a data warehouse will, however, help break down barriers and ensure, for example, that when a customer dials into a call centre, all the relevant information quickly appears on the agent's screen.

STEP THREE

Analyse the data

Once customer data has been collected, cleaned and stored the next step is to begin to make it work for its keep. In particular, to use software tools such as data mining systems, business intelligence tools and visualisation aids to sift through the data and extract useful information, patterns and trends.

Typically, companies will run queries against the customer database in order to break it up into smaller segments. For example, a store manager might want to find out what the best selling lines are on Fridays, or whether people who buy brand A also tend to buy brand B. Buyers might want to find out what are the top selling colours in men's shirts. And the strategic planning department might want demographic information that will help determine the site of a new store.

Data mining tools can also reveal hitherto invisible or unexpected patterns. Perhaps the most famous example comes from the US where Wal-Mart discovered that sales of beer rose on

Fridays if the stock was positioned next to the disposable nappies. This was because fathers tended to do more of the shopping on Fridays than at other times of the week.

More generally, data analysis enables companies to identify customer segments within the data. For example, a financial services company probably needs to know the age profile of its customer base in order to tailor products to meet the different requirements of different age groups. As customers become increasingly demanding and discerning this becomes ever more important.

Towards bespoke service

The holy grail for any customer-focused company is to tailor a product or service offering for a market of one. In other words, be able to identify an individual customer and know enough about their likes and dislikes and hopes and fears to anticipate their needs and tailor products to meet them and do so in a timely fashion.

Some of the most sophisticated data analysis tools will also enable a company to reduce customer "churn" by anticipating a customer's decision to defect to a rival. The need for such tools is highlighted by the KPMG study, which found that 43 per cent of companies could not identify the principal causes of customer churn, even retrospectively, and almost half were unable to identify customers on the point of defection.

Now, however, some telephone network operators use these types of tools to sift through call patterns and predict which customers are most likely to move to a competitor. They can then offer these customers alternative deals that may meet their requirements more exactly.

Financial institutions, telephone network operators and others can also use these techniques to spot unusual customer behaviour – for example, the fraudulent use of a credit card or the theft of a mobile phone – and minimise their losses.

Customers' lifetime values

Many companies would also like to be able to work out customer "lifetime values". These may turn out to be quite different from a "snapshot" view.

For example, a snapshot view of two bank customers might suggest that the one who always keeps a small positive current account balance is more desirable than the customer who frequently goes into the red. However, a more detailed holistic view of the two customers might reveal that the "positive balance" customer writes a lot of cheques, queues up in the local branch to withdraw cash from a teller twice a week and never uses his bank credit card. In contrast, the other bank customer turns out to be a recent graduate with high earning potential who pays only the minimum payment on his credit card each month and frequently dips into the red generating overdraft fees.

Armed with this additional information, the bank might decide to try to encourage the first customer to move to an account that charges a monthly fee in order to defray the costs of his frequent visits to the local bank, and to offer the second customer a larger overdraft, low-cost mortgage and life insurance. If the bank is really smart it will probably also suggest a meeting with one of its personal financial planners and adapt its ATM system to offer overdraft increases within prescribed limits.

Ultimately, becoming a customer-focused company is about using data to differentiate between customers and creating goods and services that more closely match their requirements.

Chapter 3

Acquiring and targeting customers

Good customer relationship management can create substantial shareholder value say William Mellis CRM partner at Ernst & Young and Mathew Stewart, executive consultant in Ernst & Young's CRM practice

Is CRM just another concept and "buzzword" dreamed up by management consultants to justify their fees for doing the same as most good marketing, sales and customer service functions? How many organisations can say that:

- *They only acquire profitable customers;*

- *They keep the customers they want to keep;*

- *Their customer-facing resources are correctly allocated;*

- *They build all the value they can into the exchange points with their customers.*

HOW CAN CRM HELP TO TARGET NEW BUSINESS?

With every communication with a customer there is the opportunity to create or destroy customer value. Latent sales potential exists at every "touchpoint". The touchpoint may be a direct request from a customer to place an order. A customer may hint at an implied need during a conversation, or simply impart information which assists with sales qualification. Even customer complaints reveal genuine data about individual customer needs, preferences, attitudes and behaviours.

So what happens to this information? Most of it is lost as soon as the telephone is put down, the meeting is over, or the e-mail is deleted. If the information is retained, it is held in the mind of the sales representative or account team member, rather than being shared more widely. In most companies there is no corporate or institutional memory where this information can be stored and accessed, in order to help large teams or disparate individuals to think and act like a single salesperson.

CRM closes the gulf between a company and its customers. It enables the company as a whole to think and act in the way a single salesperson would. The left hand knows what the right hand is doing, and therefore relationships can be built and strengthened.

Customer-driven companies face a choice: they can treat every customer communication as an anonymous transaction, or as part of a co-ordinated ongoing relationship. However, few can sustain the first position for long – in a competitive environment, if a company is not actively looking after its valuable customers, it is creating an opportunity for its competitors.

WHAT DO WE MEAN BY RELATIONSHIP?

Can we really speak of companies having relationships with their customers? Human relationships are based on many attributes, some of the most important being recognition, mutual respect, trust and continuity.

Relationships between customers and companies require the same foundations. If a customer always spoke to one particular company representative, relationships could develop naturally. Since, however, most companies are composed of many people performing different functions, it is inevitable that customers will find themselves in contact with more than one employee.

To maintain the relationship, a company must capture as much relevant information about that customer as possible, and make it available to all agents who are likely to be in contact with him or her, whether salespeople, teleworkers, engineers or appointed intermediaries.

Customer information is the lifeblood of the relationship and the key ingredient of CRM. Without information there is no recognition of the customer, no continuity between each contact and little opportunity for mutual respect or trust to develop.

IS NEW BUSINESS VITAL TO MOST COMPANIES?

The combination of challenging growth targets, intensifying competition, and the advent of new channels means that sales and service resources are stretched as never before. This situation is exacerbated further in the consumer sector by rising customer expectations and declining loyalty. In the quest for new business, firms cannot afford to distribute their sales resources blindly.

While a pipeline of new business is vital, the focus is shifting from volume to yield. How can sales and marketing resources be better targeted to achieve more of the company's strategic goals? Managing sales and marketing yield is becoming the basis of competitive advantage.

CRM tools enable individuals and sales teams to record and track the opportunities they are currently chasing. These opportunities can be consolidated into a pipeline, or sales funnel, of highly visible sales activity. The organisation's resources can be targeted and focused on the most promising opportunities with the most valuable customers.

Having visibility of the sales funnel enables companies to forecast sales, as well as spot wider changes in the market. The funnel supports team-selling, by making visible the current status of the opportunities being pursued. The data in the funnel provides the means to reward sales people for activities other than actually making a sale. For example, salespeople can be rewarded for generating sales leads for a new product, even if the sale is closed through another person or activity.

The successful companies of the future will not focus on the sales performance of individuals, but rather on how individuals help optimise customer value.

TARGETING EXISTING CUSTOMERS

The economic value of every business derives directly from the number, profitability, and duration of its customer relationships. In fact, at the most basic level, there are only three ways to increase customer value: acquire more (of the right) relationships, increase the profitability of existing relationships, and sustain those relationships over a longer period. The past decade has been filled with talk about both "becoming more customer driven" and "creating shareholder value". Despite the rhetoric (and efforts in many companies), we find that the value exchanged in the customer relationships of virtually every company are still significantly below par.

HOW COMPANIES MISS OUT ON CUSTOMER VALUE
Companies miss out on value in the following four ways:

Ineffective exchanges
Management may contribute the wrong things to certain customer relationships, resulting in those customers giving only a fraction of their possible value to the company. For example, not all customers will value the free advice they receive through account-based selling.

In these situations, it may be possible to keep the overall amount of investment the same, but change the type of investment to earn a greater return. In other words, these customers may be willing to behave differently if they were given a different type of value, ie. service upgrades, special discounts, or improved features.

Inefficient exchanges
Alternatively, management may invest more than is necessary in some customer relationships. Many times, managers can lower the amount of investment in these relationships without losing value returned. Examples of investments that are often inefficient are grocery coupons and hotel courtesy packages.

Inappropriate exchanges
Management may also invest inappropriately in relationships that currently yield poor value in return. They hope that investing more will improve the situation. However, when examined closely, it often becomes clear that for a significant segment of these customers no value exchange could be designed which would provide shareholders an adequate return on their relationship investment. Sometimes it is better to cut your losses.

Inadequate exchanges

Finally, management will invest too little in relationships that have great potential value. In these instances, it is often possible to increase the investment and receive a handsome return on the resulting customer behaviour changes. A commonly inadequate exchange is that of the inbound service call. Seemingly innocuous requests such as an address change or a request for a copy invoice, can reveal implicit customer needs which, in the right hands can be developed into clear sales opportunities. A successful "sales through service" strategy, however, requires investment in new product variants, new skills and excellent customer knowledge.

OPTIMISING VALUE EXCHANGES THROUGH CRM

Most companies do not explicitly manage their customer relationships in the way they would manage processes or products. There is no financial rigour, and little consideration of how scarce resources should be allocated so that the value exchange between customer and supplier is optimal.

With the advent of CRM tools, however, it is now possible to adopt a direct, disciplined, enterprise-wide approach to optimising value exchanges so as to close the gap between the current customer relationship and the optimum. Companies can define and segment their target customer bases and quantify the current and full-potential value of these relationships, and identify the investments most likely to realise that potential value. They can then exploit emerging flexible manufacturing processes and innovative delivery techniques to meet differing customer needs and expectations.

For a company to achieve this, management must do more than just turbo charge a traditional marketing function with information and technology, or reengineer their production and delivery processes. They must commit their entire companies to closing the full potential gap by designing and installing an integrated, enterprise-wide approach based on optimising value exchanges. This will involve rethinking four elements common to all business models: positioning strategy, investment management, delivery processes, and employee alignment.

The first step is to articulate your value exchange positioning. Broadly speaking, this involves asking which customer needs will you serve, for which target customers or segments? What core capabilities and business requirements are necessary to create full potential relationships with those customers, and how well do your capabilities align?

Going deeper, companies can begin to develop a value exchange investment management process by building a detailed, segment-by-segment understanding of the economics and drivers of their customers' behaviours. This requires developing a rigorous, quantified set of answers to the following questions:

■ *What is the net present value of changing customer behaviours at the margin?*

■ *How do customers break apart into segments?*

■ *Which customer segments exhibit behaviours that have a significant value gap?*

■ *How large is the full profit potential of each consumer segment?*

■ *What types of value drive profitable behaviours for each segment?*

■ *What relationship investments deliver the value that will most likely change the behaviour for segments with large profit gaps?*

■ *Which non-performing investments can be reallocated?*

This knowledge can help companies define and plan investments that will help to optimise the exchange of value between their customers and investors. It gives management the tools to decide where to spend limited shareholder funds to create maximum value for valuable customers.

Instead of each functional silo looking only as far as maximising the efficiency of its specific area, everyone works collaboratively to optimise the overall design of the exchanges. This disciplined process is the only way to ensure that a company delivers real value to each customer, in the most profitable way.

Chapter 4

Retaining customers

Future success increasingly depends on in-depth knowledge of existing customers. Andy Coates, principal consultant of KPMG's customer management practice, explains how CRM techniques can achieve it

Most chief executives today recognise the identification and retention of profitable customers as a top priority. Nonetheless, an alarming number of them do not understand enough about customers and customer behaviour to develop good CRM strategies. *Knowing Your Customer*, a 1999 research report on customer information by KPMG, found that the following statements are a reality for over 50 per cent of major UK businesses:

■   *We can't tell which customers are at risk of leaving;*

■   *We can't identify the principal causes of customer churn even after customers have been lost;*

■   *We are not sure who our most profitable customers are and therefore don't know which ones matter most to our business;*

■   *We don't know where tomorrow's competition for our customers is coming from.*

Such lack of knowledge is a serious problem. The reasons to get to know your customer, to understand what makes him or her tick, have never been more compelling. The breakdown of traditional industry sector boundaries means the competition is getting tougher. Established brand names are entering new markets: customers can now, say, get home and contents insurance from Kwikfit or a mortgage from their local Sainsbury's.

In addition, new technologies are providing more opportunities for a wider range of businesses to contact competitors' customers directly. The competition is literally just a "click" away.

THE CUSTOMER

Customers are increasingly prepared to shop around and compare products and services between suppliers. Add this to widening market choice and price transparency and you have all the ingredients to generate customer "promiscuity" – a willingness to buy almost anything from anywhere. In this environment, the successful companies will be the ones that identify and retain their profitable customers and nurture them.

There are three principal reasons why customers defect:

■ *"Curiosity" – the customer moves through their own choice to try an alternative offering;*

■ *"Competition" – the customer is enticed through the result of a rival's action; and*

■ *"Complaint" – the customer takes their business elsewhere because they are dissatisfied.*

Companies need to use CRM to mitigate or remove these threats to retaining their customers. But what are the CRM techniques that achieve high levels of customer retention and in what kinds of organisational cultures does CRM best thrive? To answer these questions, we need to define some of the principles of good CRM.

DEFINITION

Retention is about a company sustaining a relationship with its most profitable customers. In addition, where appropriate, it is about increasing the "wallet share" of those customers who are less profitable today and turning them into the higher value, long-term customers of tomorrow.

It is not, as is often thought, about introducing loyalty schemes, customer satisfaction surveys, price discounting and chasing every or any customer. These tactical devices can provide some short-term benefit, but are not in themselves sufficient to address the basic retention issue. Without being deployed in an integrated CRM context, they are at best often only neutral and at worst counter productive to potential future relationships.

IDENTIFYING PROFITABLE CUSTOMERS

It is impossible to meet all customers' needs all of the time, which makes prioritising customers according to their current and future value essential. Common sense dictates that if businesses are to survive they must meet the most important needs of their most important customers. Judging who those customers are is not just about crude measures such as spend and creditworthiness. The aim is to differentiate according to forecasts of an individual customer's overall profitability across a defined "lifetime".

Customer value analysis quantifies in financial terms a customer's propensity to buy and propensity to lapse and his or her "referral value" to other customers. The results are then offset against the customer servicing costs for each product to arrive at a customer profitability calculation. The conclusions can be surprising. A case in point involved a large retail bank that had spent a number of years targeting business from a prestigious client. It was only after undertaking a customer value analysis that the bank found that this client had never been profitable.

Understanding a customer's lifetime value and on-going profitability through customer value analysis will compel an organisation to think of a customer as an asset. The organisation will then start naturally to think of managing the business in terms of managing that asset and optimising it.

SEGMENTATION AND TARGETING

Once the profitable customer profiles have been identified and mapped to a business's customer base the next step is to segment those customers in order to better target marketing, sales and service activities. It is essential that businesses understand the nature and behaviour of their customers in order to be able to tailor their products, services and means of interaction.

Segmentation means placing customers in groups that respond to and interact with your business in similar ways. This contrasts with the traditional approach of dividing the consumer market by socio/demographic groups and the business market by size and sector. Today, organisations need to take an approach that is directly relevant to the business they are in and to the customers they wish to serve and retain. A more holistic understanding of the customer is required – including buying history, personal preferences, lifestyle and personal circumstances. This information is a pre-requisite to ensuring that marketing spend and activity are effectively targeted and that the right products are offered to each customer at the right time within acceptable economics of delivery.

Volvo, is a prime example of the use of this precision marketing, actively targeting cars and car products at the growing family by understanding relevant lifestyle issues.

CUSTOMISATION

Typically, marketing and sales activity is geared to selling the same product to the mass market. Although differentiation based on segmentation recognises the diversity of the market, it does not recognise the individual needs and preferences of each customer.

The information needed to provide a company with the insight into the real needs and preferences of customers often exists, but is difficult to find and is therefore rarely used effectively. Companies need to direct sufficient resources to the sourcing, accessing and processing of this customer information in order to generate the kind of knowledge that will drive the innovation process to customise products and services. The development of products and services has to be refocused on those that are tailored to individual customer needs. In its successful quest to supplant Mercedes in the US market, Lexus (the luxury car brand of Toyota) sent a group of senior executives to experience the American way of life and used what they learned to influence its range of vehicle designs.

CROSS-SELL/UP-SELL

Provided that a relationship can be maintained with the customer and that the right information is available to the organisation at all the relevant customer contact points, the opportunities to increase or repeat the sales of an existing product, or sell additional products and services to that same customer increase. An organisation is able to anticipate specific customer needs and target an appropriate dialogue or activity at the right moment. Through good CRM, financial service providers such as banks, insurance companies and building societies have been able to link mortgages, home loans, contents insurance, car loans, car, travel and health policies and investment products. The focus here is on maximising customer or wallet share, which is more profitable and, with the right customer information, easier to achieve rather than market share.

CUSTOMER SERVICE

Successful companies make conscious decisions about the level and quality of service they wish to develop and sustain. Others let it evolve or, worse, have no consistent delivery process at all. Commercial carrier businesses such as DHL have set and promoted specific, high service levels, and delivered according to them.

The sensible company recognises that different customers have different service requirements. Customer preferences can differ widely. Some people, for example, are happy to communicate with a company via the internet; others prefer the telephone; others face-to-face dealings. Some customers only feel comfortable talking to someone in whom they have already established a trusted relationship; others can be more flexible.

Companies that focus on one type of customer can design their service provision around the most common preferences. Those with a broader client base must either vary their methods according to preferences common to specific customer groups or offer every-one a free choice. The key point is that the decision should be based not purely on cost, but reflect customer preferences, be consistent across all means of interaction be brand aligned and reliable.

SERVICE BRANDING

Developing a brand around customer service may be one of the most difficult tasks in marketing and indeed may not be appropriate to many types of business. It is about creating a customer affinity with the style and means of service. Brands are usually associated with specific products rather than the way an organisation relates or interacts with its customers.

Any service can be branded if marketing messages are developed and communicated to targeted customers. However, it will not be customer service oriented if the messages focus on price, product performance, or incentive "gifts" sent to people looking to buy. Customer service can be used to support a brand's campaign to differentiate itself from the competition. This is particularly true if the proposition of the brand is to appeal to a group of people with special service needs. First Direct, for example, has made a big business out of the principle that telephone banking can best serve the needs of busy people.

ORGANISATIONAL CHARACTERISTICS

There are some familiar features of organisations that achieve and maintain high levels of customer retention. These characteristics tend to transcend industry sector, product type and customer base.

The first of these is lack of complacency. The organisations that manage customers well are never in stasis. They constantly review and reassess their customers, products and services, and the next potential source(s) of competition.

Companies that take this approach have also recognised that in developing the products and services that their customers want, they themselves do not have to create all of the value. Partnering, alliances, acquisitions and brand relationships can help in the development of new products and services that truly reflect customer demand and so engender loyalty. This has been demonstrated by Kimberley Clarke and the selling of its Huggies nappies. The company looked in detail at the everyday needs of the mother and developed a definitive range of related products with 21 leading brand partners. It now dominates the market over its nearest rival, Procter & Gamble.

Typically, such companies are also keen to invite comment and feedback from their customers and learn from it. A significant aspect of Cable & Wireless's high-profile brand marketing campaign was the invitation to customers to "tell us what you want".

Much has been written elsewhere about the largely unproven relationship between customer satisfaction ratings and revenue generation. The annual customer satisfaction survey that is often cumbersome and inflexible can leave the customer feeling they have done their account manager, rather than themselves a favour. Creating the ability to have a true dialogue with customers requires courage and the readiness to change once the customer has spoken. Hewlett Packard, for example, took the step of inviting a significant number of its key customers to review its end-to-end operation and implemented many improvements as a result.

Companies that are good at CRM also recognise that the value that their employees place on the customer is directly proportionate to how much value the company puts on its employees. Learning, empowerment, accountability and the encouragement of initiative again require courage but reap dividends.

CONCLUSION

Most companies remain ill-prepared for an increasingly competitive environment. There is general recognition that a company's existing customer base is the key to its future. However, many companies are still particularly poor at using the techniques and technologies available to capture customer information, understand it and use it effectively. The reasons are principally cultural. "Silo" thinking prevents the cross-functional sharing of information, hampering the ability of companies to:

- *View the customer in a consistent manner;*

- *Understand where the valued and profitable business lies;*

- *Target their activities appropriately;*

- *Adapt their products and services to meet customer needs;*

- *Deliver to the market with a high standard of customer service;*

- *Operate seamlessly.*

The winners in the battle for customer retention will be those who can apply CRM to satisfy customer curiosity, differentiate themselves from the competition and open a genuine dialogue over complaint.

This could be the breath of fresh air your company needs.

For more information please contact
Andrew Coates, KPMG Consulting on 0207 311 1000.

www.kpmg.co.uk

KPMG

It's time for clarity

Chapter 5

Growing customers

Customer information is one of a company's greatest assets. Waste it and you waste the chance of competitive advantage says Kelvin Spratling, head of Oracle UK's practice business intelligence and data warehousing consulting

Most established companies are sitting on a seam of data about their customers' demographic profiles, their preferences and buying habits.

Effective CRM involves using this information to build customer loyalty. The organisation can identify its most – and least – profitable customers and those whose circumstances, lifestyles and spending patterns indicate that they are ripe for further development.

NEGLECT OF INFORMATION
The travel industry provides one of the best examples of how the opportunities presented by information are being neglected. When customers book holidays, they give their names and the names of their families, their addresses, their ages and other personal details. If this information is used at all by travel agents, it is simply to save retyping if the customer visits the branch again.

But the data the customer has given includes useful demographic information. Postcodes, for example, show what area customers come from, the kind of house they are likely to live in and therefore what income bracket they may be in. The choice of holiday gives a useful indication of their preferences, how much disposable income they have and how willing they are to spend it. Do they book early, paying the full list price to be sure of getting the holiday they want, or do they leave it until the last minute and take whatever is going cheap? Are they prepared to pay extra for a room with a seaview? How much do they take with them in currency and traveller's cheques? The travel industry's customers continue to provide valuable information as they check in at the airport, arrive at the resort and book excursions with the local rep. Do they take advantage of the half-board they have paid for or eat out most evenings?

This information, if collected at all, is likely to sit in a number of disparate databases, rather than being drawn together in one place where it could provide a full picture of the customer's dealings with the company. Assembling such data and storing it in a consistent, accurate and accessible way presents challenges, but the tools and skills to do it are available.

WINNING COMPETITIVE EDGE THROUGH DATA

Most high street travel agents offer a similar range of holidays, often from the same brochures. There is little incentive for the customer to go back to one rather than another, unless the experience of booking a holiday has been a memorable one.

Instead of simply sending out a brochure, the travel agent could look at the customer's history: where they've travelled to, what kinds of holidays they've booked. Perhaps there's a new hotel in the same or a similar resort with a kids' club to give the parents more time to themselves.

The agent could assemble a choice of holidays based on what he knows about the customer. He could also use the information he has to refine the way he interacts with the customer. Questions such as, "Are you still at the same address? Will the children be coming with you this year? Would you like a room with a seaview again?" will give the impression that the company has taken care. And if they have been offered a selection of holidays suited to their tastes and requirements, why should they take their custom to an anonymous agent down the road?

Mass-market travel companies can use the information about what excursions the customers have taken to begin to compete with the niche suppliers of wildlife, historical or similar specialist-interest holidays, offering a package that combines, for example, a couple of weeks' trekking with a week in a beach resort.

NO SUCH THING AS BAD INFORMATION

The more information companies have about customers the better. "Bad" news is better than no news. Most travel companies treat complaints like thorns in their sides and deal with them on a one-off basis, without making further use of the information. Handled effectively, a complaint can present an opportunity to build a better relationship with the customer – for example, by offering them an irresistible deal the following year. Customers whose complaints have been met with concern instead of indifference and been dealt with satisfactorily can become more loyal to a supplier than those who have simply experienced the day-to-day, "ordinary" services.

Complaints can also expose weak links in the supply chain, leading tour operators, for example, to demand better performance from hotel keepers and other suppliers, or to employ new ones. Sometimes, problems can be solved by rewriting promotional material: if the brochure does not raise false expectations customers will be less likely to be disappointed. Accommodation that to a family might seem spartan and lacking in entertainment facilities might be just the thing for a self-styled independent traveller. It is a question of targeting.

IMPORTANCE OF CONSISTENCY

The customer database needs to be fully integrated so that however the customer makes an approach – in person, over the phone, by post or via the web – the same information about them is available. Once that database is built, the company can begin to segment its customer base to focus its marketing. Obvious categories in the travel industry are singles and couples aged between 18-30, families, and the over-50s.

Business information tools can be used to identify patterns, to see what segments are ripe for expansion by direct marketing and to see how branches in different towns are performing with respect to those segments. The business information tools should be flexible enough to allow the marketing department to interrogate the data from any angle. This can then be used to produce the customer profiles on which the database depends.

USE OF DATA BY SUPERMARKETS

Supermarkets have a better record of using the data they collect on their customers, for example, through loyalty card schemes. But in recent months the effectiveness of these schemes has been questioned, with Asda withdrawing from its scheme altogether. The truth is that most customers' wallets are stuffed with such cards and that the supermarkets are not doing enough to identify and develop their most profitable customers.

All supermarkets need to know is in the contents of the shoppers' baskets. Are they buying baby food and nappies? Would they respond positively to offers on other baby products? Have they been buying more expensive wines, but neglecting the range of cheeses the store offers? Vouchers for particular products could be awarded along with points to encourage them to try new lines.

Store credit schemes require customers to give details of their salaries, their financial commitments, and other store accounts they hold. All this information could be combined with their buying histories to determine whether the right products are on offer at local stores. The data can be collected, analysed and made available overnight to individual stores so they can react quickly to changes in buying patterns. It may even be possible to adapt offers and prices to meet the changing profiles of customers at different times of the day and week. Most pensioners may visit on a weekday morning, after collecting their pensions; most working couples on Thursday or Friday evening; most families on a Saturday.

This kind of customer profiling has been done for years by market traders, who raise their prices to catch workers shopping in their lunchtimes, then drop them again for people looking for late afternoon bargains. The only difference is that a street trader can do in his head the sums he needs to make a profit.

CUSTOMER QUESTIONNAIRES

While Data Protection legislation restricts to some extent what an organisation can do with the information it collects on its customers, questionnaires, backed up by incentives like prizes or vouchers, can be used to persuade the customer to provide information voluntarily. Restaurants could – as Cafe Rouge already does – offer a free bottle of wine in exchange for filling in a short questionnaire.

The internet presents a viable alternative to the traditional market researcher in the street with a clip board, or thick forms sent by post. Web questionnaires can be tailored almost in real time, to refine the questions being asked, or to follow up an emerging trend.

UNFULFILLED POTENTIAL OF THE WEB

Some 17 per cent of UK households now have internet access, but retailing over the internet is still in its infancy: too many websites reflect the organisation's internal ordering systems, rather than presenting customers with the high powered graphics and easy navigation they have come to expect. The sites also make little use of customer histories to personalise their offerings. If you regularly buy books on IT from Amazon.com, for example, you may ask yourself why Amazon doesn't offer to take you straight to the IT listing when you log on.

Similarly, if you go direct to the site of a travel company you have used before, you may wonder why you are not being guided through a menu tailored to your previous choices.

Few companies track the behaviour of customers visiting their websites. The majority might leave the site at one particular page, for example. Why are they doing it? Is the price too high, the interest too limited, or are there simply too many levels of screen? Would it be more effective to put the most successful pages nearer the front, or to mix in the less visited pages with the more popular ones?

Amazon.com has been successful in offering customers online access to the status and progress of their orders. DHL offers a similar service. As well as giving customers a sense of being in control, these WISMO (where is my order?) systems can result in process improvements and savings for the supplier who can cut down the number of people handling telephone queries.

But such systems will only work if the customer-facing systems are properly integrated with back office purchase, accounting, stock and logistical systems. Too many businesses see CRM as an add-on to their existing systems. Really successful companies, like

DHL, use customer relationship management to combine customer loyalty and service with improvements in business processes. Well-designed CRM systems create an expectation that back-end processes must be able to fulfil.

COLLAPSE OF INTERNAL INFRASTRUCTURE

Once upon a time, banks were able to lock in their customers by making it very difficult to move their accounts. The rise of telephone banking has made moving accounts easy. CRM is a way of making your customers stay with you because they want to, not because they have to. If your service is efficient, polite, and tailored to their needs – so that they can quickly and easily amend a previous order, instead of spelling the new order out from scratch – why should they look at your competitors, even if they are cheaper?

We are now seeing the rise of internet businesses with little or no infrastructure other than a CRM system. Design, manufacture, warehousing and delivery, invoicing and payment handling are all outsourced. This could be what the future holds for many suppliers – distributors and other middlemen may see their businesses threatened by disintermediation of the supply chain.

Chapter 6

Customer insight

The technology now exists for companies to have business-critical data at their fingertips. But, says Philip Blackwell, director of CRM at Cap Gemini, it is only as good as those who use it

Customer knowledge is vital for survival and growth in today's competitive environment. The customer should be treated as the font of all knowledge in formulating a successful CRM programme. The customer is king. Organisations must understand who their customers are and how to hold on to them.

These statements may seem obvious and a merely matter of common sense. Many companies, however, are not sufficiently focused on gathering information on customers or on using it effectively to meet changing customer needs.

It is a lack of direction they can ill afford. Changing lifestyles mean that customers have less time, and require information on and access to products and services 24 hours a day. Companies need to satisfy this demand and retain customers who are loyal and profitable. It is imperative that they identify who their key customers are and know what they want.

GAP BETWEEN THEORY AND PRACTICE

Recent global research by Cap Gemini found that although most companies understand the importance of customer knowledge few of them are actively involved in improving knowledge-gathering processes and systems.

The research revealed that for the majority of companies the core objective of a CRM programme is to improve relationships with the existing customer base. There is a strong business case for doing so: statistics show that keeping an existing customer costs up to 10 times less than acquiring a new one.

Other key aims are to provide a personalised service for the customer, to differentiate products and services from competitors and to identify the most profitable customers. Cost reduction and gaining new customers are not ranked as key objectives.

Companies now, more than ever before, have the potential to fulfil the theory of effective CRM in practice. An increasing range of tools is available to them. The technology to improve customer knowledge and information is available and is constantly becoming more sophisticated. It includes internet/intranet technologies, data warehousing, data mining and predictive modelling techniques.

For the companies that make good use of the new tools, the benefits can be huge. Greater understanding of customer groups is allowing companies to target new products and services better and facilitating brand-stretch initiatives. Tesco and Boots have both been able to move into new areas such as financial services and travel insurance partly through improving their customer databases.

THE IMPORTANCE OF INTEGRATION

For the real prizes to be won, however, gathered data must be integrated; it must be available throughout the organisation and consistent across all units. Such integration leads to three levels of understanding: understanding of the business; of the business processes; and, of course, of the customer.

The process of integration is not always easy. Sometimes, the data is stored in "legacy" or "heritage" systems that do not "speak to each other". Sometimes, it never travels between departments because of internal communication problems. (Marketing and finance, for example, may have historically kept what they know to themselves.) Sometimes, it is not shared between different channels – such as a bank branch and its web site.

The true worth of the customer to the business can only be determined by looking across all business units and at all channels and customer "touchpoints". Customer management can be counter-productive if the customer's true value and, ideally, potential value, are not understood throughout the organisation.

So, in an ideal world, relevant information from across the

business should be available to all functions and channels and be collected from all functions and channels. This information should then be used in a co-ordinated and integrated way to ensure that there is a single, consistent view of the customer throughout the organisation. The customer will then receive a more efficient service and be left with the feeling that the company is genuinely concerned about his or her personal requirements.

Consistency of response is vital. The disparate parts of the company must be able to give the impression of being a whole – of being the single company or brand the customer has a relationship with. After all, this is how the customer views the company.

DISSEMINATION OF INFORMATION

For the results of data collection to be deployed effectively, they must be thoroughly analysed and carefully managed. The insights gained must then be fed to all the channels where there is customer interaction. For example, an insurance company planning a direct marketing campaign should ensure all its customer service agents are well informed of the campaign and ready to meet increased demand or answer customer enquiries effectively.

So to create a CRM strategy that works, the whole picture should be considered and manageable steps planned. The prerequisites for success are:

- *A single customer view throughout the organisation;*

- *Effective data management considering data synchronisation, technical architecture and data quality;*

- *An analytical capability using people and tools, including automated tools where appropriate;*

- *Carefully thought out methods of deployment – eg. campaign management, channel integration;*

- *Continuous learning to gain further insight from results;*

- *Cross-functional people and processes aligned to the CRM strategy.*

MODELS FOR GOOD CRM

The insurance sector, which is well advanced in using new technologies to gather information on customers, offers useful models for effective CRM.

In the mid 1990s Wesleyan Assurance, for example, decided to undertake a review of its entire business. Wesleyan knew that its customers were ageing and that it would have to attract and retain new ones. It had other serious problems: its sales people – who were also having to act as doorstep premium collectors – were leaving and its average premiums were too low. It was also bogged down in unnecessary paperwork. Wesleyan decided on a radical updating of its traditional sales and customer processes, underpinned by IT. The system to support the new process, known as FAITH (Financial Advice In The Home), also featured built-in compliance checks and the power to effect underwriting at the point of sale.

The introduction of this new customer-friendly technology and totally revamped sales process has produced dramatic benefits. Annual revenue has increased by 30 to 40 per cent, productivity has risen by 100 per cent and sales force turnover has decreased from 30 to 15 per cent. The company has also been able to improve service, giving instant, accurate replies to customer enquiries.

Wesleyan's experience shows how good CRM is indistinguishable from good business practice. By better management of its customers relationships, the company has built a better business. Part of the reason for its success is that it took a holistic approach to CRM. It realised that data collection is only the first step on the ladder to winning and retaining customers, that it is what you do with what you know that counts.

TECHNOLOGIES TO ANALYSE INFORMATION

In the coming decade, the insurance sector is likely to have a huge requirement for strategic analysis of customer information. Cap Gemini research has found that the number of insurance companies intending to invest in data collection, or "warehousing" initiatives, will grow from 20 per cent to 79 per cent within two years.

In response to the industry's need to manage customer information effectively, an international consortium, including Cap Gemini, Sun, Oracle and KiQ, recently launched the technology Omega+. This technology offers the relatively new technique of predictive modelling. This uses the past actions of customers to anticipate their behaviour. It gathers information on how customers have interacted historically and then makes use of it when dealing with the rest of the customer base. For example, insurance companies can identify the customers most likely to close their accounts and target them in preventive action.

Another practical example of the benefits of predictive modelling can be seen from its use in retention and growth marketing campaigns. By predicting which customers are more likely to respond to cross-selling, an insurance company can focus its communication and reduce cost.

Omega+ also tackles the high failure rate (up to 80 per cent) of traditional data warehousing projects in the insurance industry. This failure rate was largely due to a "big bang" approach: companies tried to introduce a single, company-wide project, rather than tackle the problem in more manageable phases. Often, the project was anachronistic by the time it was completed: in the two or three years that it took to build the database, the organisation had forgotten or changed its original objectives.

Omega+ gets around this problem as it is scaleable. It introduces the concept of data warehousing in a small environment, where it is tested and controlled. From the results of this, the business case is put together.

FROM PRODUCT TO CUSTOMER FOCUSED

The automotive industry is another sector where resources are being successfully invested in CRM. Volvo, which employs more than 75,000 people in 20 different countries and has production plant sites across the world, has refocused its strategy to move to a customer-oriented culture. The car maker realised that to target the right markets it required information about individual customers and "families" of customers – for example, golf players

– rather than broad market segments. Customer information existed in many different national and central IT systems but it was not linked. Volvo decided to create a company-wide customer database system that allowed customers to be tracked as they moved within a country or between countries and that supported marketing campaigns.

The company used a multinational project team from Sweden, the UK and Holland to devise a customer database that meets the aims of building better customer relationships and selling more cars.

CONCLUSION

Customer knowledge and insight is linchpin of successful CRM. Without this knowledge being shared and used throughout the company, projects will fail to meet the constantly changing needs of customers.

Starting with the gathering and analysis of relevant information, companies can move on to complete the CRM jigsaw successfully and reap the resulting business benefits.

Chapter 7

Interacting with customers

CRM tools can enable companies to build intimate relationships with those who contact them. Andrew Sutherland, Oracle's practice director, advanced technology solutions (EMEA), explains how to use them to best advantage

The mass production and mass marketing of recent decades have had huge operational benefits, lowering costs and making production more efficient. But, in the battle to win and retain customers, companies are now trying to reverse one of their effects: the impersonalisation of service.

Commoditisation means better service is increasingly seen as the main way to differentiate yourself from the competition. Companies can differentiate themselves by a branding strategy or by paring down costs but both these strategies have drawbacks: the former is very expensive, the latter can reduce profits and make a business vulnerable to competitors who have access to cheaper materials and labour. The services you provide around your product could be a better way of winning competitive advantage.

Instead of being regarded simply as consumers, customers are increasingly seen as part of a virtuous circle of product and service development. A business must capture information on customer demands in a way that can be used by marketing and product development teams.

DIFFERENTIATION THROUGH INNOVATION

Supermarkets are particularly vulnerable to commoditisation. For many people, the question of where they shop comes down either to convenience and location, or price. Once all supermarkets begin trading over the web (Iceland is already claiming to be able to reach 97 per cent of its UK consumers via its web and telephone shopping services), the choice of supplier will simply be a matter of price – unless, of course, innovative ways are found of interacting with the consumer.

Suppose, for example, a food retailer, with the customer's consent, fits a fridge with a combination lock to the outside of a customer's house. The retailer stores the customer's regular shopping list and delivers either on the customer's preferred day of the month, or when an intelligent device in the customer's larder or fridge indicates that foodstuffs need replenishing.

(Many different IT and communications companies are working on "intelligent fridges" and similar appliances.) Why in these circumstances would the customer then buy from any other supplier? This is customer lock-in for positive reasons – very different from the historical approach of banks and utilities, which forced "loyalty" from their customers by making it difficult for them to transfer to another supplier.

The new method of interaction should, wherever possible, involve the customer in making fewer explicit choices. With the customer's agreement, the supplier can monitor the customer's activities and build up a profile of requirements. An obvious example is keeping a record of the customer's shopping list, so that they simply have to add or delete the variable items before sending off the order.

THE APPLIANCE OF TECHNOLOGY

To achieve this kind of close and complex relationship, businesses need to be able to interact with their customers intimately. The technology to enable businesses to interact with each and every customer personally is already available. But it must be applied as part of a coherent CRM strategy.

Choice of technology will be crucial. Companies should be able to offer as many channels of communication as their customers demand. Channels should be directly related to the lifestyle, requirements and preferences of individual customer groups.

Whatever the method of interaction used by the consumer – a call centre, the internet, a hole-in-the-wall machine, interactive television, a multimedia kiosk, a mobile phone – consistency from the company is vital. The supplier's message should not vary from one channel to another without good reason. It may decide to offer lower prices on internet shopping to persuade more customers to use the service. But customers should not find, before or after making a purchase, that lower prices are available via another channel simply because someone forgot to update a database.

Different channels have different strengths, and different costs. Clearly, the company will want to spend as little as possible setting up the channels, or "re-purposing" content for different media. Its approach must be based, however, not just on cost implications but on its knowledge of its customers. Is one channel to be primary and, if so, which one and why? Or does the business want to provide equal access across all channels to satisfy the full spectrum of customers, from those who insist on personal contact with a company contact before making a major financial commitment to those who spend most of their working lives travelling and so need to communicate mostly by mobile phone?

IMPROVING E-COMMERCE FUNCTIONS

It is important that businesses recognise that the internet is not, of itself, the answer to everything. It gives a much greater depth and richness of information that can be communicated to the customer – even at a great distance – but there will be occasions when swapping over to a call centre, or going to a branch, will be better.

"Many e-commerce functions report a high number of abandoned transactions. Linking the call centre to the web site to provide agent interaction capabilities is likely to help convert many of these browsers into buyers," says the IT analyst group Datamonitor. "Incorporation of self-help facilities, along with agent-web interaction, can lead to improved customer retention."

Web-integrated call centres are suited to the handling of complex products of high commodity value, and particularly important for helpdesks and sales-order taking.

CUSTOMISING INTERNET SERVICES

Any discussion of the internet and customer service must inevitably include the concept of a portal. Originally, this referred to services like Yahoo, which offer a search engine, giving access to the entire internet. Now large organisations are beginning to offer their own portals. A portal is much more than just a fancy name for a website: in the true sense, it is a doorway to an organisation, giving access not just to information but to business processes, a single place to which the customers come to interact with the business. There is much that can be learned from the major internet portals and how they customise/personalise navigation and content.

Web sites can supply accurate and up-to-date information about the customer and fuller and richer customer profiles. What time of day do they like to do business? What level of technical competence does their interaction with the website reveal and can this be used to tailor or target services to them?

SELF SERVICE AS ADDED VALUE

The internet is also increasing opportunities for self service. At its simplest, this can be a direct analogue for shopping at a physical store – the customer pushes a virtual trolley around a cyber-mall. At a more sophisticated level, customers can be given the opportunity of tracking the progress of deliveries online, at any hour of the day or night. (Companies such as DHL already offer this service.)

Increasingly, too, the internet is providing a virtual help desk for clients of of software companies: customers can find the answers to common problems online, without the cost and delay of waiting for and speaking to an agent over the phone.

But self-service must offer the customer a benefit. If a company is simply pushing work onto its customers, the strategy could backfire. There are real opportunities to deliver value with digital goods and services. For example, if a customer installing a new printer finds they need a new software driver, they can go immediately to the supplier's website and download it – instead of dialling a US 1800 number and waiting six days for a floppy disk to arrive.

A business that can identify this kind of value for its customers can use self service both to increase the loyalty of its customers and to cut costs.

COST ADVANTAGES OF INTERNET SERVICE

The internet also has a part to play in billing. It can cost between £1 and £3 to bill a customer using the mail; presenting the bill electronically costs a fraction of that. But the internet is more than simply a cheap alternative to the post.

Along with the bill, a telecommunications company could provide management information tools that enable the customer to identify why, for example, the current bill is higher than the last one, and where savings could be made. A higher risk strategy would be to give the customer the means to make price comparisons with competitors.

Offering management information and other services could justify charges for the billing service. "In order for billers to realise a return on investment from Electronic Bill Presentment and Payment (EBPP), customers must shift from paper-based to electronic methods of bill presentment and payment," says Beth Barling, author of *Electronic Bill Presentment and Payment: Creating Opportunity from Necessity*, a report published by the analyst group Ovum. "Billers in most regions need to encourage customers to go online, perhaps by offering incentives."

Making the customer pay for EBPP services is a cultural issue. In most cases, pricing models for EBPP are likely to follow the model for on-line banking services. In the US, customers expect to pay for bank services, including paying bills. Will retail customers in the UK follow their example?.

"Our forecasts indicate that critical mass of customers willing to adopt EBPP should be achieved by the middle of the next decade," Barling continues. "With over 30 trillion bill payment transactions per year, even a relatively small shift to EBPP will represent a huge opportunity."

An internet billing service that offers information and other services can also act as a portal, lead to cross-selling opportunities.

CONCLUSION

Interacting with customers as individuals over the appropriate channels provides an opportunity for a virtuous circle of product development, driven by customer requirements and demands. As interactions with the customer become more intimate, customer loyalty should increase. Ultimately, every business should be looking to develop personal relationships with each and every customer. In time, as "mass customisation" techniques become more sophisticated, it should be possible to tailor products and services exclusively for every customer.

Chapter 8

Improving service through systems integration

Technological obstacles are preventing companies from developing fully collaborative relationships with suppliers. Dennis Howlett, business writer, explains why, in the interests of customer service, they must be overcome

In recent years, the ability to use software to help with supply chain planning and scheduling (SCP) and supply chain optimisation (SCO) has taken on increasing importance.

The purpose of supply chain applications is to provide management with the means of smoothing out production so that finished goods are delivered according to scheduled plans and that, where revisions to the plan have to be made, disruption is kept to a minimum. Ultimately, then, they are part of a company's strategy to deliver a better service, product and relationship with the customer. In an optimised system, value is delivered to the enterprise by eliminating waste and pruning production costs. Techniques such as just-in-time inventory planning are part of that equation, but the over arching concept centres on delivering customer value.

EXAMPLES OF SUPPLY CHAIN MANAGERS

Industries that benefit from SC applications are many and varied but the best examples come from the high technology sector. These are characterised by a need to fulfil orders at a fixed price, in a market where margins are razor thin and where consumer prices are continuously falling.

The computer maker's problems are complicated by the rapid pace of technological change and because individual component prices are volatile. This means that makers that keep a lot of stock lose out when upgrades are introduced and when prices fall. The ideal inventory position is zero: no manufacturer wants to be left with old, out-of-date stock on which it cannot make a profit. The ability to respond rapidly to changing market conditions differentiates the winners from the losers. Thus Dell, which sells PCs directly and controls its own inventory, has succeeded where companies such as Compaq, which uses resellers, have lost out.

EFFECT OF THE INTERNET ON SUPPLY CHAINS

The impact of the internet is a major driver for extending the notion of supply chains. Some commentators believe the effect of the internet will be so profound that, in the near future, it will not be individual enterprises that compete but supply chains.

DIY retailing is one sector where this could happen. Today, the market is dominated by a few big-brand retailers that in turn rely on thousands of other household names for their stock. The goods suppliers themselves rely on the retailer to provide the economies of distributed sales that keep profits healthy and order books full. The internet has the potential to change the relationship between suppliers and shops from one of collaboration to one of competition. The suppliers, for example, could decide to try selling direct to the end customer, increasing their distribution costs but improving their profit margin. To maintain the collaborative relationship, the retailer may have to offer incentives to the suppliers. These could take the form of helping to manage production and distribution plans and so improve profitability.

INTEGRATION PROBLEMS

At this point of further collaboration, one immediately hits an IT brick wall. While major enterprises either standardise on packaged applications or use their own tried and tested systems, the likelihood is that each member of the supply chain will be using different software. What differentiates one software vendor's products from another is not functionality but application design. It is an established fact that integrating any two systems is a costly, time-consuming exercise that can considerably delay required strategic changes. Experiences of creating enterprise resource planning (ERP) environments over the past five years have only confirmed this view.

However, the logical extension of joining systems is that, at some point, ERP simply has to integrate with "something else". No-one, for example, wants to go through the planning process, come out with a bill of materials and then manually re-enter the plan into another ERP purchase requisition system. Similarly, it would be nice for a retailer to dip into a supplier's plans to see how prioritising goods might assist in the product flow. Or, for the supplier to dip into the retailer's plans to figure out demand loads then automatically generate parts orders in the supplier's system. A finishing touch would be to ensure that purchase orders generated in one system are matched with purchase order requisitions generated in the other.

SOLVING INTEGRATION PROBLEMS

There are several ways to tackle the compatibility problem. The IT company SAP has become the world's leading supplier of ERP systems but it recognises it will never "own" everything. Indeed, when one looks at its real market share, it only has a small fraction of the world's ERP systems. Third party applications vendors, however, now realise that they need to integrate with SAP systems and many have developed connectors that address the majority of supply chain "touchpoint" problems. Competitive ERP vendors have done the same thing: Oracle, for example, today has some connectors for SAP systems.

Connectors are one approach; another relies on enterprise application integration (EAI) tools. These are usually appropriate where one is integrating mainframe systems and packaged applications but they could be equally useful where many disparate systems are being brought together. Integration happens at two levels. First, one needs to make sure the databases can talk to each other. Although individual approaches vary, the "hub and spoke" tool has gained significant popularity. This sits at the centre (hub), drawing in data from one or more outside sources (spokes) and then translating it into something the receiving system (another spoke) understands. At the second level, one is considering process integration. This is a thorny problem for a variety of reasons but the idea is that business processes in one system are understood by another using an intermediary tool. As yet, process integration is still beyond practical reach: it remains the ideal, however.

A third and more exciting approach is the use of standard messaging so that data coming from one system is understood independent of the second system. This does not avoid the potential need for data sharing through a hub and spoke tool, but it means that a lot of the effort needed to understand data formats is removed. It is being pursued through Extended Markup Language (XML) standardisation initiatives that are seen as non-threatening to software and platform vendors. There is real expectation among vendors that XML will provide the parachute everyone needs to get out of the integration battle. Today, it is possible to exchange e-mail messages that are understood by recipient systems and translated into business actions, but while workable, it is a crude system.

DON'T PANIC

The main thing to understand is that while integration is not easy, existing ERP users do not have to ditch what they already have and look for a supplier that does everything in a combined ERP/SC solution. That would be unwise in the extreme. If anything, organisations should think in terms of accepting where they are with ERP and, provided it is year 2000 compliant, simply stop developing it. They can then concentrate on integration strategies that provide the best means of integrating with agility.

The importance of agility cannot be over emphasised. Even though one might successfully integrate systems with suppliers and customers both up and down the supply chain, relationships change. This means that integration will become the norm rather than a one-off event. Provided decision takers do not panic and undertake the analysis of what integration can deliver, the problem becomes manageable, productive and ultimately delivers value to the business – and better value to the customer.

Chapter 9

Sales and service

Company representatives have a pivotal role in CRM. Sam Anahory, partner of PricewaterhouseCoopers' Management Consulting Services, looks at ways to make sure they fulfil it well

A few weeks ago, I received an unsolicited phone call at home from my telephone service provider. I felt better about the intrusion after the agent had informed me that he was carrying out a quick check to make sure that I was receiving the full range of discounted tariffs.

What actually happened over the next 25 minutes was that the phone agent reeled off a prepared script, asking contrived questions at various points, in a weak attempt to encourage me to buy additional services. He had no real understanding of what products and services were being offered.

This was the latest Customer Service Initiative introduced by the company in question – 10 out of 10 for good intentions, one out of 10 for actual value. Thankfully, the phone cut off and the agent never called back.

You probably have had a similar experience yourself. Many organisations are chasing a new Holy Grail: superior customer value and improved customer loyalty. Unfortunately, few are as yet employing methods likely to attain it. In this chapter, we will look at best CRM practice among those at the frontline: sales and customer service staff and company agents and representatives.

THE NEW SERVICE CULTURE

"Frontline" employees now need to operate in the context of what might be termed a new service culture. This culture involves attempts to make qualitative improvements to customers' experiences of companies. The rationale for making these improvements is self-evident: the more you sell to loyal customers and discourage existing customers from defecting to your competitors the more successful you will be. In a highly competitive marketplace, the barriers to attracting the right kinds of customers are not just related to how much you can afford to undercut competitors. Prospective customers have begun to place more value on the quality of the product and more importantly, the quality and the style of the service they receive. Pricing is important, but it is only part of the picture.

To see the bigger picture, you need only look at the way supermarkets – which once provided examples of the "pile 'em high and sell 'em cheap" culture – now market themselves. Gone are the days when food shopping was an anonymous experience. Since loyalty cards were introduced, supermarkets communicate with us on a regular basis and even actively encourage our custom. If you have recently moved house, the chances are that you will have received a "welcome pack" from the supermarket chain you use most often, helpfully pointing out where its nearest store is and providing a bunch of discount vouchers or goods to welcome you to your new home.

Supermarkets use the information they have on their customers for precision marketing. During the BSE crisis, for example, many promoted alternative meat products to people they knew usually bought beef. They could not have done this if their customers had been anonymous to them.

TOWARDS QUALITATIVE IMPROVEMENTS

A customer's perception of the quality of the service experience can only be enhanced if the same higher-value interaction occurs at every customer "touchpoint". This is why the role of company representatives and sales people is so pivotal in CRM. Consistency of response gives the customer the impression of being valued by and known by the business: they are more than just an account number, that is why they are being treated in the same way regardless of how they make contact.

Large customer call centres, where hundreds of service agents respond to customer queries, have obvious implications for the quality of the service experience. Such centres may fulfil operational requirements and lower costs but they may not deliver everything the customer wants. Vital as they are, the phrases "How can we help you madam/sir?" can get dangerously close to a bland litany.

Without real customer contact and real insight into customer lifestyles and behaviour, it becomes almost impossible to provide differing levels of service to different customers. With it, you can make your customers more loyal. If a mother with a young baby calls a roadside recovery company and is immediately asked if her child is with her it will make her feel good about the company. Crucially, it will make her feel secure: this company knows her, it appreciates her needs and is going to make her rescue a priority.

MANAGING RELATIONSHIPS BY GROUP PREFERENCES

There is a weight of evidence that indicates that customers prefer being treated as individuals, whose wants and needs are being satisfied by the customer service agent. This is particularly true when they are buying what might be termed lifestyle products. Having a disembodied voice instruct you how to order cinema tickets using the phone keypad (Interactive Voice Recognition) is one thing; having it help you decide which pension scheme to choose or what (expensive) holiday to buy is something else.

Operationally, it is can be economically impractical to give each individual customer a personalised service. However, you can create the illusion of personal service by knowing which group of customers an individual belongs to. Insights you have about groups who share certain general characteristics and propensities can be applied in particular contacts. It is important, however, to remember that sometimes less is more. Mobile phone users who call a customer service desk with billing enquiries, for example, are likely to want prompt attendance, not a long speech on tariffs etc.

In summary, the customer service experience can be enhanced, by providing:

■ *A consistent customer service experience at all customer touch-points within the organisation. (The company's message should be: "We know you and treat you the same way regardless of how you interact with us".)*

- *A more personalised service experience designed to appeal to that consumer, using segment-based customer insights and propensities to drive the interaction with the customer.*

- *Service experiences appropriate to the expectations of the customer, ie. not embarking on a 20-minute conversation when the customer is after a two-minute transaction.*

The sales experience is enhanced if the customer believes that he/she is being provided with a personal service. In effect, the sales agent can engage the customer on the products and services that may be appropriate to him or her, as indicated by the insight and propensity information.

The old sales technique of concentrating on the benefits of the product or service to the consumer still applies. Thus the customer's initial response of "you are going to sell me something" becomes "what a good idea, you're making life easier for me".

CREATING REAL CUSTOMER VALUE

Customer information in itself is not sufficient to create customer value. It is the way the information is exploited within the business that matters. One of the most common ways of creating value is by making sure specific customers receive the appropriate level of service, ie. communicating with a customer on the basis that they wish or would like to communicate with you. Some people may not wish to be bombarded with "special discounts" or other promotional material, but would value a service that is more convenient and hassle free. Others may be price conscious, or looking for a product or service that is innovative or removes drudge.

Valuable customers expect to be treated differently from less valuable customers. Customer contact strategies that exploit this differential have tended to increase the perceived quality of customer service. Reinforcing customers' sense of self-worth – saying "you are important to us" – reduces customer churn.

If the customer is assured of being provided with the same level of service whenever he/she deals with the organisation, their sense of being valued will be deepened even further.

Technological advances mean that companies are able to know more about a customer's buying habits than ever before.

Over the next few years we will see much more sophisticated exploitation of customer information. Walk into your regular supermarket and the assistant at the meat counter could say: "How was the Sunday roast you had last week? I've put aside a fresh cut which I'm sure you'll enjoy; and by the way, we would like to offer you a bottle of claret to enjoy with your meal as a thank you for being a loyal customer."

THE STEPS TO BETTER SERVICE

What practical steps must you take to create the "total" CRM organisation? The first thing to achieve is a single customer view. Without it, we cannot be certain we are dealing with the same individual in the same way. Accuracy of information is of paramount importance. If the same individual appears on your database in different ways – eg. As Mr A. Smith,.Mrs A. Smith, Mr A. Smyth, Mr A. Smuth – you're immediately in trouble. You have to examine the database carefully and eradicate any errors

The second step is to keep detailed records of what each customer actually buys. Affinity programs (eg. Sainsbury's Reward Card, Tesco's Clubcard) and home shopping programs (e.g. Iceland Home Shopping) provide obvious mechanisms for doing this. The information gained can be used to create a much better understanding of customer needs, to drive forward, or even create, a new retail proposition.

The next piece of valuable information is the customer contact history. Every customer contact should be retained for analysis to refine the model of customer behaviour. This can have the benefit of saving company time and sparing the customer unnecessary hassle. If you know that a customer has been approached once to purchase a new product or subscribe to a new service and refused you may decide not to bother him or her a second time.

The insights you have about customers are used to inform the last and most important stage: scripting the customer interaction to achieve the result you want (cross-selling, up-selling, perceived improvement in customer service, etc).

Technology is used to ensure that when a customer calls, they will be automatically put through to the most appropriate person to handle

THE STEPS TO BETTER SERVICE

the query. If this agent has a full record of all previous interactions (ie. customer contact history), the customer will be more likely to receive the appropriate level of service.

The agent needs to understand what kind of customer he or she is dealing with in order to maximise the value of the customer interaction. This understanding is achieved by displaying segmentation and insight information about the customer to the agent who is handling the call, or the account manager who is having a conversation with the customer.

The information could include:

■ Propensity to defect to a competitor;

■ Potential reasons for dissatisfaction with the service/product;

■ Likely response to cross-selling and up-selling;

■ Indications of lifetime value and value to date.

This information can then be used to drive the interaction (through dynamic scripting). The agent/account manager should be picking up the interaction where the last agent left off and focus on the things that add value to the particular customer.

The technologies now exist to make this information available. Examples of them are: computer telephony integration in call centres, web-enabled contact histories on laptops or personal digital assistants and, more mundanely, customer interaction scripting at an EPOS (Electronic Point of Sale) checkout.

Chapter 10

People and culture

The quality of a company's relationship management is determined by its culture and ethos and, ultimately, by its staff. Geoff Lock, business writer, looks at how true "information communities" are born

CRM depends on, and is driven by, state-of-the-art information technology. However, it can only succeed when supported by a corporate culture that understands and is aligned to customer-focused objectives. In short, your board, your corporate HQ and, crucially, your people, must be on your side.

If you're thinking of getting involved with relationship management as part of your strategy for the future, think carefully about what you're trying to do. Getting together all the information that you have about customers past and present is an excellent idea. However, reaching the stage where you are both collecting the knowledge and making it available across the whole organisation is not a straightforward task. And it could ultimately depend on fundamental cultural change.

BLIND FAITH IN TECHNOLOGY
The technology of CRM delivers mechanisms for collecting, classifying and retrieving information about customers. For it to work effectively, however, there has to be a working environment in which openness is genuinely valued: individuals must be prepared to make their own knowledge available to the wider group.

IT provides almost limitless opportunities for using information, but can guarantee nothing about its quantity or quality.

"Everybody sees the advantages of technology, but few see the disadvantages," says Adrian Payne, director of the Centre for Relationship Marketing at Cranfield University. "Even if a management has been made aware of disadvantages, it's too easy to see the positive side, without understanding the drawbacks. The problem usually comes in the implementation, as technology and people need to work together."

Companies often demonstrate an almost irrational faith in the power of technology, blinded to the importance of other things. In his recent book, *Information Masters,* John McKean suggests that companies typically put 80 per cent of a programme's investment in technology when the ideal figure should be closer to 10 per cent (see table). The weight given to IT means all other aspects of the programme become starved of resource.

HISTORICAL INVESTMENT vs. IDEAL INVESTMENT		
ELEMENTS	**HISTORICAL INVESTMENT**	**IDEAL INVESTMENT**
People	2%	20%
Processes	2%	15%
Organisation	2%	10%
Culture	1%	20%
Leadership	1%	10%
Information	10%	15%
Technology	82%	10%
Total	100%	100%

Adapted from John McKean's book, Information Masters

DANGERS OF HIERARCHICAL STRUCTURES

"CRM depends on trust, co-operation and open working relationships," says Richard Scase, professor of organisational behaviour at the University of Kent. "It needs lateral communications that work by virtue of the fact that they cut across hierarchies. Organisations are traditionally segmented, with reward systems still based on what you do in your part of the organisation."

Creating openness in the workplace is probably one of the hardest things to achieve as it involves major changes to "soft" aspects of the working environment. People, processes, organisation, culture and leadership (all those things that in the past have been given low priority) may all have to change. And given that there is usually resistance to change, this might be thought an insurmountable obstacle. But, provided the exercise is approached with care, fundamental cultural changes can be made.

UK companies have historically been organised on a strongly hierarchical basis, in which there is a pecking order and many grades through which employees can progress. Reward is based on rank and rank in the company confers status. As human beings, we seek status, quite often without knowing it. Within a work group, status comes both from position and from possession of knowledge – the two often, but not always, coincide.

CRM and other techniques based on openness introduce conflicts and complications because the information with the greatest commercial value may be held by staff with the lowest rank. Usually, there is neither any incentive nor any mechanism for collecting and using that information. For its value to be realised, however, the information has to be shared. This leaves companies in a predicament that is the direct result of their working culture – a culture that has evolved over decades.

CHALLENGING THE OLD CULTURE

"Older styles of management are based on assumptions about how to get the most out of people," says Dr Rob Yeung of business psychologists Nicholson McBride. "A lot of early work on motivation assumed that employees are intrinsically lazy, unambitious, irresponsible and not to be trusted. Management styles took this into account and not surprisingly, when people are treated as irresponsible and lazy, they respond by becoming irresponsible and lazy, and a culture of control is the result."

Changing the way your company functions internally is not something that can be done quickly. Organisations in recent decades have been moving towards flatter structures with fewer levels of hierarchy. Moving from a traditionally hierarchic culture to one of employee empowerment, however, requires significant changes in processes and systems. New behaviour patterns have to be promoted in such a way that they are seen to be non-threatening and a desirable objective.

FIRST STAGES IN THE PROCESS OF CHANGE

"The first stage in a culture change programme is to identify the current culture by talking to people in the business," continues Yeung. "Find out what doesn't work at the moment, but also what does – so you don't risk "throwing the baby out with the bath water". And talk to people from all levels of the business. Managers and longer-serving employees will have a different view of what has and has not worked well in the past, while newcomers will have a more realistic perspective on how outsiders perceive the company's current culture."

The next stage involves canvassing people at all levels of the business to determine what the new culture should look like. By giving people an opportunity to contribute to shaping the future direction of the company, it encourages buy-in and gives staff a psychological stake in the project.

For it to work, however, the project must be given right status within the company – otherwise people who need to be involved won't be released from their normal duties. Some might find working on a project like this challenging as it will be very different from their normal operational job, so be prepared to make the effort to help them to help you define the future direction. Getting the right input and the right degree of commitment are essential to getting the right vision.

"Any new style of management has to encourage enthusiasm," says Richard Scase. "Where people don't feel their talents are being fully utilised, both the company and the country suffer a loss of creativity and innovation." Then, as this is after all about changing to a culture of open management, you must tell people what you are doing and why, so that they understand the benefits and what's in it for them. Ultimately, you want them to change the way they behave, which is a major undertaking. It's not just about retraining managers to be nicer to employees, but putting feedback mechanisms in place so that employees can influence their managers' behaviour.

REMUNERATION AND REWARD

Once you have done this, you are well down the road to change. The most difficult and important changes are in those "soft" areas. A vital step is realigning processes and systems so that remuneration, appraisal and promotion schemes reward the right sorts of behaviour. Genuine employee empowerment should let people make decisions about their own futures, with the opportunity to contribute to the company's. Progress should be carefully measured so that obstacles can be overcome as soon as they are identified and improvements recognised and rewarded.

BE PREPARED FOR THE LONG HAUL

It's a big job and will take time. Changing culture takes twice as much time and three times as much effort as most companies estimate, so whatever you do, don't give up. The biggest danger to projects like this is that they outlive the normal lifespan of a management team. Resist the temptation to clear out all projects that haven't been completed when a new team takes over – otherwise, all that investment will be wasted and morale will be seriously damaged. Some companies have been working through their cultural change programme for five years so far, yet are pleased with their rate of progress.

Patience and determination will ultimately be rewarded: successful introduction of CRM along with changes to culture and working methods can bring enormous benefits. Your company's place in the eyes of customers and its relationship with its employees will both change for the better. This can only have a positive effect on your position in the marketplace.

With your staff on your side using the accumulation of their knowledge and experience you'll be surprised by how much you can achieve. Have them against you and life could become unnecessarily difficult.

Move fast enough and it's nectar

nectar

nectar

These days, it's not only
what you know–it's how fast you know
it, and how fast you can get it into the right
hands. Our network of people in more than 130
countries has the knowledge to help you get
results. Together, we can move forward
faster faster faster. Start humming.

www.eyuk.com

For further information contact:
William Mellis, Partner – UK CRM Leader,
Ernst & Young 100 Barbirolli Square Manchester M2 3EY
Tel: 0161 333 2756
email: custcon@cc.ernsty.co.uk
Web site: www.eyuk.com

CONSULTING · TAX · ASSURANCE

FROM THOUGHT TO FINISH.™

Chapter 11

A smaller company perspective

CRM tools and technologies can allow SMEs to compete on a level playing field with large companies. Marc Beishon, business and technology writer, explains why

Imagine you are a smallish manufacturing firm, producing top-quality technology for large corporates in highly demanding domestic and international markets. You have only a small sales-force and your main marketing effort for both new and existing customers has traditionally consisted of direct mail and advertising.

But last year you installed a purpose-built call centre – comprising just four or five desks – and staffed it with a tele-marketing team working round the clock to make targeted calls to your customers, wherever they were in the world. Regular contact with key prospects and existing customers has led to a far better pipeline of leads to your salespeople and distributors and a level of customer satisfaction that would be the envy of many a larger firm.

Then you added a website which holds a full on-line catalogue with pictures of products and components, and allows your customers to log in and see the history of their orders with you. Coupled with your call centre operation, the website provides: a "store-front" to your firm that's as up-to-date as you like – and never goes "out of print"; a personalised experience for your buyers; and perhaps also direct on-line trading, if it suits your business model.

Ultimately, it can help build a strong community of relation-ships among supplier, distributors and resellers, customers, consultants, the trade press and so on. It has also given you the thing today's businesses seek most: competitive advantage – your two main rivals are still doing it the old way...

The difference CRM systems make is easy to see. So why do so few SMEs invest in them? To find out, you need only look at their marketing plans – or what passes for them. Far too many companies neglect marketing – particularly, relationships with existing customers. Is your insurance broker, for example, only in contact with you at that expensive renewal time – or does it keep in touch with a newsletter that shows it's keeping on top of the business?

CRM'S ADVANTAGES FOR THE SMALL BUSINESS

The examples of good relationship management are sadly few and far between. And yet, the case for SMEs adopting CRM techniques could hardly be stronger. They give small companies the opportunity to promote themselves to their customers as never before. Unlike traditional brand-building and customer retention strategies – such as above-the-line advertising – they are relatively low cost. This makes CRM one of the few areas of marketing in which SMEs can compete with big companies.

What is more, smaller companies are often better placed to develop a relationship marketing strategy: unlike large corporates, they tend not to have unwieldy computer systems containing different types of information about customers. With only a limited amount of "legacy" data, they can act more quickly to make changes.

IN-BOUND CALL CENTRES IN THE SMALL FIRM

The call centre, one of the bedrocks of modern CRM practice, is no longer the preserve of the likes of Littlewoods and First Direct. To qualify as a call centre, you need only have a handful of people employed as dedicated call takers or makers – in fact, many so-called "formal" call centres start life as informal groups of people answering and making enquiries.

Formal call centres split neatly into in-bound and out-bound operations, and there has been a revolution in the technology available to help with both. Agents working on out-bound systems, such as telemarketing operations, can be equipped with a database that not only tells them all about a customer's history, but can also prompt them to make suggestions and elicit further information, based on the client's responses. This kind of database can run on low-cost networks of personal computers, and there is a range of call centre tools now available to customise the interface to suit the work that the agents need to carry out.

Meanwhile, smaller firms are finding that they can set up equally successful in-bound call centres to take orders or service customers, with the underlying purpose of really understanding the customers' needs and spotting opportunities to upgrade and sell to their friends and business acquaintances, and so on.

A key enabling technology for the more advanced call centre is computer telephony integration (CTI), whereby customer details appear automatically on a screen as the call is taken.

REFINING THE TELEPHONE-BASED BUSINESS

A certain degree of development work is needed to take an existing customer database and marry it with a telephony solution for in- or out-bound call centre operations. Because of this, the first sectors to adopt the advanced systems have tended to be the more IT aware businesses such as recruitment agencies, financial houses, IT firms and telemarketing agencies. No company, however, will be able to survive much longer without at least sorting out the basic requirements for telephone-based business.

The first step is to undertake an audit of existing call patterns. This may, for example, reveal that a high proportion of callers hang up because they can't get an answer, or ring off once they do get through because they are passed around the company to the wrong people. It may reveal that it is time to consider a dedicated group to receive or make calls. Or show that other parts of the company are weak in relationship management terms. Customers often need, for example, to have regular contact with the technical people – the designers, engineers and mechanics – who are working on their jobs. But these employees are notorious for being away from their desks – supplying them with cordless phones integrated into the company switchboard would provide clients with a hotline to track a job's progress, reducing the number of complaints and increasing satisfaction.

The telephone is, of course, not the only channel to your customers – although it has become perhaps the most important and powerful one for many firms. A CRM strategy can also support traditional face-to-face meetings with salespeople and visits to a customer's premises by your personnel. So-called salesforce automation tools can vary in sophistication from a simple contact manager to a full-blown presentation system that can show customers a tailored solution, based on the latest product and client data that firms hold in-house. Getting the members of the sales team "on-side" in a relationship strategy is important: their knowledge can be better used if it is captured in a system rather than being kept in their heads.

CRM IN THE FIELD

Consider, too, the opportunities when, for example, service engineers visit customers. Equipping field personnel with a decent job scheduling and location system not only means that appointments can be kept or rescheduled by just an hour or so, but also that opportunistic work can be covered. If Mrs Smith's washing machine breaks down and you know you have a technician working in the next street, it may make good sense to do that job next – and Mrs Smith may well tell all her neighbours how happy she is that you did.

Staff who spend a lot of their time on customer premises are also in an excellent position to make formal or informal enquiries about the quality of service and the performance of products – the opportunities to gather the information that could improve relationships and lead to "up-selling" are clear.

THE EVOLUTION OF E-COMMERCE

There are other elements of the CRM mix, such as direct mail, advertising, exhibitions, workshops and public relations, that need to be assessed and used in the right way for a business. It is, however, by no means easy to decide what weight to give each one: so much depends on the number of customers, the value of certain customers, and the type of business.

What is certain is that the channel everyone's talking about – the internet – will become hugely important and exert a huge influence on CRM. Indeed, some analysts are already redefining CRM as a subset of the newer concept of "electronic relationship management". Taking steps now to plan how you can build up your presence on the web are bound to pay dividends. Most UK firms, if they have an online presence at all, use websites mostly for passive information or strictly as a place to buy and sell products and services. But they can do much more in CRM terms.

CUSTOMISATION OF WEB SERVICES

A website offers a special ability to tailor a relationship to suit a customer, so that whenever they visit they see only those products, promotions and messages that you want them to see. What's more, you can hook up that interface to their history of buying from your company, so that they themselves can see what they bought last year and order the same again – without needing to know the exact part number or specification.

Installing this kind of web technology can provide a superior form of CRM precisely because it puts the customer in the driving seat. It fulfils one of CRM's key aims, which is to give customers access to all the services from your company that interest them, in a user-friendly way.

Recognition of the value of this type of service has prompted companies such as Federal Express to allow customers to track the progress of parcels in real-time. Meanwhile, electronics distributor RS Components has developed a site where each customer has their own welcome page showing tailored editorial, advertising and new product alerts relevant to each customer. And a raft of British craft firms has set up sites showing pictures of their latest products – anything from teddy bears to sausages to cakes – so that a customer in Chicago knows exactly what they are getting, and that queries are answered promptly by e-mail.

Most people know by now the mantra of the internet – it's a great equaliser for the smaller firm. Nothing illustrates this more than its potential to fulfil CRM aims. Via a website, a small firm has the same opportunity to build a relationship with a consumer as a big company.

Chapter 12

The future of CRM

Mass production and mass marketing have created the need for a new business model. CRM tools, says Paul Taylor, IT correspondent of the Financial Times, will help build it

It is often tempting to dismiss "new" management concepts as just the latest business school fad – or another ploy by marketing men and consultants to plunder the corporate coffers. But there are plenty of reasons to think that CRM is different. A recent study by Spikes Cavell found business managers believed CRM had the potential to transform business performance by:

- *Lowering the cost of customer acquisition;*

- *Retaining customers for longer;*

- *Creating more opportunities for cross selling;*

- *Giving a company the ability to behave like a new entrant.*

Perhaps the most powerful argument for taking CRM seriously, however, is that it is mostly common sense.

CRM is about putting the customer back at the centre of an organisation's activities and using technology to rebuild the sort of relationships local bank managers or corner shop owners had with their customers 30 or 40 years ago. Then, these businesses had real, lasting relationships with their customers, relationships built up over years of face-to-face contact and personal transactions in the context of local knowledge, in the context of pieces of inform- ation that told them about their customers' lives. As a result, they could make informed, sensible and timely decisions that helped ensure that customers remained loyal and reasonably satisfied.

Unfortunately, these old-style distribution models were very costly to run and often rather inefficient and have mostly been replaced by more automated systems. The newer models rely less on expensive manpower but deliver bland and relatively rigid "one-size-fits-all" goods and services, often remotely.

MASS MARKETING AND ANONYMITY

Mass produced products and services are not designed specifically for anyone; the hope is that they will be sufficiently attractive to a broad but largely anonymous audience. In many cases, suppliers of them will have little or no direct knowledge of the end customer – they may not even know who their customers are. These mass-produced goods and services represent the opposite of the "bespoke" tradition – they are low cost but also low value. The inevitable result has been a dramatic decline in customer loyalty, now identified as "churn" in many industries, much higher levels of customer dissatisfaction and a marked reduction in the level of trust between clients and service providers.

Crucially, many companies are now competing with increasingly commoditised products, and the only differentiator is the customer relationship. These problems have been compounded by several other factors. Not least among them is the rise of electronic commerce. In the internet world especially, competitors are often just the proverbial "mouse-click" away. What is more, they may be new competitors from an entirely different industry. In many businesses, such as financial services and telecommunications, barriers to entry have virtually vanished, resulting in a flood of new rivals, offering goods and services at a price and quality that have turned many sectors into commodity markets.

SHIFTS IN THE BALANCE OF POWER

When there was little or no supplier choice, customers were forced to accept second-rate service. But market liberalisation, the shift to global competition and the commoditisation of many products and services have changed the balance of power between suppliers and the customers – and these consumers have high expectations. At the level of customer behaviour, brand loyalty appears to be a dying concept.

There has been a real power-shift from manufacturers to

consumers and, as the new generation of net-savvy children become consumers with real buying power, this shift is unlikely to be reversed. Meanwhile, the cost of new customer acquisition is skyrocketing, as the task of shouting above the noise of competing offers becomes ever more difficult.

According to some estimates, it costs five to eight times more to acquire a new customer than it does to retain an existing one. Other startling statistics include the calculation that companies generally have a one-in-two chance of selling a product or service to an existing customer, but only a one-in-16 chance of selling to a customer with no previous relationship.

ANACHRONISTIC BUSINESS MODELS

For these, and other, reasons, there has been an upsurge of interest in concepts such as CRM, "mass-customisation" and "the market of one" over the past year: more and more companies have realised that the conventional mass production model on which consumer marketing has been based no longer works. "Companies across the world recognise that to survive in an increasingly global and competitive marketplace, strategic focus on the customer is critical," said a recently published Andersen Consulting report prepared by the Economist Intelligence Unit.

At the same time, instead of focusing narrowly on cost-cutting measures and improving efficiency, a growing number of market leaders are re-examining their business strategies and deciding that, in the internet era in particular, customer service and customer relationship management are the keys to future growth.

In order to implement better CRM strategies, some companies have begun to break down existing internal cultural barriers and build centralised data-warehouses containing a wide range of customer information gleaned not just from transactions, but also from many other sources. This is often not as simple as it sounds because many organisations have multiple customer databases – sometimes with different departments controlling access. Even so, building a common customer database is often at the core of an enterprise customer management strategy, which will typically also encompass sales support, marketing support, customer support – including call centres – and quality assurance.

Companies are then using the increasingly sophisticated tools available from IT vendors to segment customers, target the most profitable and improve the quality of their customer relationships; and they are exploiting new technologies such as interactive kiosks, digital television, the web and call centres to expand the range and quality of their customer interactions.

Crucially, they are beginning to take a holistic view of their customer relationships and focus on the lifetime value of those relationships instead of just a "snapshot" view.

Know the customer; target the customer; sell to the customer; and service the customer – these have become the new imperatives of industry and commerce.

ELECTRONIC RELATIONSHIP MANAGEMENT

The recognition that it is time to take CRM seriously has coincided with a switch in emphasis by many organisations from back-office systems such as enterprise resource management (ERP) to front-office systems and enterprise customer management (ECP) or customer relationship management systems.

In the process of corporate restructuring – downsizing etc. – that took hold in the past decade, particularly in the US, many companies lost sight of the customer. For them, the real question now is: how are we going to increase revenues while still keeping costs in line?

What is beyond doubt is that the market for software that helps manage customer relationships is hot. According to industry analysts the CRM market is currently growing at more than 40 per cent a year.

Looking forward, however, both CRM vendors and their customers face some challenges. One of these will be to integrate the new front-office and customer relationship management systems with existing legacy and back-office systems. But some analysts also believe that CRM systems themselves will need to be adapted to take account of the growth of the internet and web-centric applications and will evolve into what has been called "electronic relationship management" suites.

Using these ERM suites, companies will dynamically link together different sales and distribution channels and connect all their business partners, including suppliers and resellers, into what has been dubbed a "proactive information rich e-relationship" environment by Forrester Research, a US-based IT consultancy. Forrester argues that this will further accelerate sales and streamline customer support.

THE 360-DEGREE VIEW

What is already clear, however, is that managing customer relationships today is about more than simply automating a sales force. As the database specialist Oracle notes, it is about putting the strength and skills of an entire organisation behind every interaction with the customer – from the time a company first begins to market its products and services, to flexible tailoring of a service contract or making sure the latest and most complete customer history is at the fingertips of the person answering the telephone.

It is about increasing customer satisfaction and reducing the number of customer defections by collecting and analysing information across marketing, sales, service, and other parts of an organisation in order to provide a true 360-degree customer view and then aligning resources with customer needs. It is about improving market reach and customer loyalty by implementing the most appropriate customer interaction strategy, whether it's through the web, a call centre, a direct sales force or third parties.

Finally, it is about expanding revenue opportunities and customer satisfaction by developing more personalised relationships with customers and partners, resulting in more effective sales and service relationships and building true one-to-one relationships by harnessing integrated information from all customer "touchpoints". In other words, it is about using technology to turn transactions into relationships.